A Crash Course in Coalition Building:
Easy steps for mobilizing a community.

Acknowledgments

When you have a loving and supportive family like I do, it seems anything is possible. Through the ups and downs of life, they have remained a steady constant. For that, I am grateful. I dedicate my drive to write this book to my husband, three sons, my sister, and her beautiful family. Without you, I am nothing.

I dedicate the inspiration for this book to the community of Miami County, Indiana. Everyone within this community deserves acknowledgement, as they are the ones who grew with me, and continue to give me the strength to work for change.

I dedicate all the in-betweens to my closest friends. Thank you for being you! I must acknowledge my "ghost member". She continues to reminded me not to be complacent, and always plan the next big move.

Table of Contents

PREFACE

CHAPTER 1- GETTING STARTED

CHAPTER 2- YOUR FIRST MEETING

CHAPTER 3- BEING PREPARED

CHAPTER 4- THE BIG DAY

CHAPTER 5- NOW WHAT?

CHAPTER 6- LOW HANGING FRUIT

CHAPTER 7- ASSESSING COMMUNITY NEEDS

CHAPTER 8- IMPLIMENTATION AND STRATEGIC PLANNING

CHAPTER 9- GETTING TO WORK

CHAPTER 10- CREATING POLICY WITHIN YOUR COALITION

CHAPTER 11- SUSTAINABILITY

CONCLUSION

Preface

When considering an organizational leadership position, one must understand that it is not a role for the weary. While the potential success of the objective at hand can be exciting. There is a certain amount of drive one must possess to reach desired success. This drive almost always comes from the intrinsic hunger to change the outcome for another person in the way one wishes was done for them. As you will learn, it was this hunger that drove my aspiration to work toward change.

My journey begins nearly fifteen years after experiencing the social services world first hand as a 14-year-old runaway. I could not have predicted myself in a professional setting or engaged in collaborative change with the very system I felt failed me. I earned a degree in the science of psychology and was hired as a home-based service provider. My employer was a state-wide, not-for profit organization contracted through the department of child services. This role put me on the front lines, assisting clients with employment, housing, parenting, and any other requested objectives. This task, at times, could be most daunting. The lack of resources available made some situations nearly impossible to overcome.

Through this work I learned several of the most valuable lessons of my career. Entering the lives of strangers at a low point, changes your perspective on life. In the lives of these clients, I was exposed to the severity of their addictions and their needs. Because of this exposure, I was determined to take what my clients deemed their worst experience and turn that into an educational opportunity. An educational opportunity they could use long after their case was closed.

It was in this desire to educate that I found myself seeking collaboration with other organizations. With no formal training, I approached both traditional and nontraditional entities that would make a positive impact on these individuals' lives. I looked for organizations and community support I could lean on after my job was complete. These organizations varied from the local YMCA to a used car dealership. Each organization had a valuable lesson to teach, whether in quality family values or finance.

Eighteen months passed quickly while searching for transportation with families without funds, applying for employment with fathers hiding felonies, and wiping countless tears of the hopeless and defeated. I began to search for more. I wanted a position that would allow me to dedicate 40 hours per week, 52 weeks a year to families. I wanted to provide the support to families that I went without as a teen.

I searched the employment pages for what I now know to be my dream job, Local System Coordinator. In these pages, you will walk through a step-by-step guide on how I am able to create and sustain an organized group of diverse, creative and passionate individuals from multicultural backgrounds. With this book, you will facilitate the change you desire within your own community.

Chapter One: Getting Started

Now that you have the opportunity to coordinate, organize and lead your community to positive change, where does one start? This is a question anyone in your position asks on more than one occasion. This chapter, "Getting Started" is designed to walk you through, step-by-step on where to begin the task at hand. You do not have to follow these steps in exact order, but it is recommended. This guide will help prevent you from making the mistakes I made and provide you with a head start in your effort.

First things first

Day one is the day you have been waiting for at your new position. Expect a meeting with your new supervisor to discuss where s/he would like you to begin. Your head will be spinning, adrenaline rushing, and hopefully your writing hand is rested. Your supervisor is going jump right in, knowing there is no time to waste. Right out of the gate s/he will throw out names, meeting times, stories, and so on, with the expectation it is being absorbed in your overexcited brain. Take a deep breath and follow the steps below.

Step 1: *Listen, listen, and listen.* Listen for names, committee meeting dates, hints of political agendas between organizations, and anything else your supervisor requires you to do. With this position comes a lot of freedom, but your supervisor will still expect you to fulfill items on thier agenda as well. It will feel like a whirlwind of obligations in the beginning, but you must jump in and use those organizational skills you most likely added to your resume.

Step 2: Write, write, and write: Your supervisor is saying something important, so write it down. Write down every name, add a small brief on who they are and why they are important. This step is especially critical in the event your supervisor requests you not contact someone or that they be included in a meeting. Be mindful that the community in which you are working is political and requires a collaborative dance toward fulfilling individual agendas.

Step 3: Questions, questions, and more questions: Have you ever heard the saying, "The stupidest question is the one you do not ask?" Apply that right here, in this step. In the middle of all the names, dates and obligations your supervisor will most likely stop and say, "Do you have any questions?" This is where you say, "Yes."

Below are some critical questions to ask. You can always add to the list.

1. Are there any individuals or agencies that have a history of not collaborating well with each other? Why?
2. Are there any questions that should not be asked to specific organizations? Why?
3. What is the schedule and communication expectation for the position? How much freedom do I have?
4. Do I get business cards? These are critical to networking.

5. Do I get reimbursed for meals purchased for monthly meetings?
6. Are there any meetings I must attend? Do not need to attend at this time?

Step 4: *Process, process and process*: The meeting with your supervisor is over. S/he sends you off to process the information. Take your notes back to the office and create a "drawing board." Whether this be formally written notes or a cork board with all your new tasks, you need to organize and structure the information you have received. Re-evaluate the notes, add what you remember but could not write in fast enough and then organize them. You want to choose an organizing technique that suits your needs and one you can maintain over time.

Typing your notes will help the information stay tidy while driving it into your long-term memory.

It is important you read the material and process all that was said. The details are important to your success. If you have a gap in information, go back a step and ask your supervisor. Do not let critical information go undocumented. This could have negative consequences in the future.

Step 5: *Plan, plan, and plan*: Take the time you need to process and organize the information you receive from your supervisor. Now is the time to plan. The best way to approach this would be from the inside out. Identify all formal, professional, and internal support first; then begin looking outside.

Why identify internal support first? These individuals have a vast amount of knowledge and are waiting for your call. You may not think they are, but they are. By arranging a meeting with each one of these individuals, you will be furnished with information, points of contact, resources, and ideas on how to approach the next stage of your journey. By building strong support for yourself early you will not feel alone on rough days to come.

Things to remember:

1. Get permission to complete all the internal meetings. This could take two weeks. Your supervisor may want to know what you are doing with your time. If you present this plan to them, you are most likely golden. Be sure to document who you met with, the date, time, and length of each meeting. This information is needed for monthly tracking or report writing, goal setting, and will keep you organized.

2. If your support team suggests any good books to read. Be sure to read them. It is important you learn the lessons they are trying to teach. Gather as much insight as possible. Try audio books to listen to the material suggested as it allows for multi-tasking and note-taking.

Learn about your community

Once you have completed the internal meetings and organized the information provided, it is time to broaden the circle. Again, you are working from the inside out. So now it is time to focus on the community. Take what you have learned in the past few weeks and apply it to learning every square inch of your surroundings. The following steps will guide you through learning your community's history and creating a community assessment using both secondary and first hand data. By doing this, you will piece together the strengths and weaknesses within your community.

Why complete this time-consuming task? As a coordinator, you want to educate yourself as much as possible on the community. This will engage you in conversations within the community, and guide you to appropriate programing in the future. If you chose not to partake in this step, you may regret it.

Step 1: *Secondary data collection*: Data is the key to any community assessment. Being able to provide factual numbers to those receiving this information is crucial. People want facts and so do you. Since you have not ventured out into the community yet, secondary data is a good place to start. Once data gaps surface, venturing out for first hand data within the community is only appropriate. Below are suggestions as to where secondary data can be found.

Secondary data locations: U.S. Census Bureau, state health department, department of agriculture, bureau of labor statistics, recent community needs assessment statistics (these may come from larger organizations within the community), state and government websites.

Step 2: *Data collection from local organizations*: Once you have recovered as much secondary data as possible and have successfully identified data gaps, it is time to collect more, but from within the community. This data is collected directly from the source and is the most current data. You may have to compile this data yourself to get the needed statistics. Below are suggestions as to where the most current data can be found.

WARNING- This list is much longer than the secondary data list.

First hand data locations: Local law enforcement agencies, city and county schools, local hospitals, probation department, family services, court appointed special advocate (CASA), community liaisons, the local United Way office, city hall, mental health agencies, substance abuse treatment providers, the juvenile court system, the county jail, prosecuting and defense attorneys, coroner's office, drug task force, special education providers, early education providers, adult education providers, and families in the community.

Now, as you can see, this is a long list and involves meeting a lot of people. Before you set out on a mission to collect this data, read the suggestions below as to how this can be done with ease and success.

Suggestions on collecting organization data:

1. Research each location on your data collection list.
2. Locate the director or supervisor of the department storing the data, and her/his contact information.
3. Create an introductory e-mail. State who you are and why you are contacting her/him. This is an opportunity to attach any information to further

explain your objectives and goals. Make sure this e-mail is introductory only, and includes a request to meet in person.

4. Add "read receipt" to these e-mails to ensure the correspondence was opened and the information received.

Tip: These are the stakeholders you need on your coalition. Be sure you are professional and openly clear about your objectives. Transparency will allow them the opportunity to decide if they wish to help you with your objectives.

Sample of an "introductory" e-mail:

Professor Jones,

I am Sarah Sawyer, Program Coordinator for Johnson County. I am delighted to say that I have an opportunity through the America Social Service Association (ASSA) to assist in the building of a coalition focusing on substance abuse and mental health treatment within the community. I have met with several professionals to discuss the needs of Johnson County. Are you available to meet and discuss your assessment of our community and its needs? Please contact me at your earliest convenience. I greatly appreciate it. I can be reached at (123) 456-7898 or via e-mail.
Thank you.
Sarah Sawyer, BS

Once you receive a response and s/he has agreed to meet, schedule a meeting. Allow between 90 minutes and 2 hours for each meeting. Use this time to ask her/him about their organization, how s/he feels about the issues at hand, and your community assessment. Simply inform her/him of what you are working toward. If you feel as though s/he is receptive, this could be a good opportunity to ask if s/he could help you locate data.

REMEMBER: This is your first impression, and a time to be professional BUT be yourself. Trust in who you are and keep relationship building at the forefront. These individuals see a lot of faces, and you want them to remember yours.

Send a follow-up e-mail after each introductory meeting. Thank the individual for her/his time and interest in your cause. Some of the individuals you meet are more than busy, so this step cannot be skipped. Remember, you are trying to build a diverse group of individuals and work toward change. These are the individuals who can make that happen.

Sample: Thank you e-mail:

Professor Jones,
   Thank you for meeting with me on Tuesday. It was great to hear about your organization and the efforts you are involved in. I would enjoy meeting again and updating you on my progress.
Thank you again. I hope to see you soon!
Sarah Sawyer, BS

Step 4: Compile all data: Analyze all the data you collect from your requested sources. This is how you begin to build the community assessment document. If you are unable to process the data independently, go to a local community college and ask for assistance from a professor.

By the time you complete the data compilation, which includes all data, the document will most likely be between 8–10 pages. Check and re-check all the data. Read the document in full to ensure it flows successfully. Provide a well-constructed document to whomever requests it.

"Community Assessment" or data compilation structure: History, demographic information, education, employment, income level, minimum wage, SSI recipients, those receiving Temporary Assistance for Needy Families (TANF) recipients, food assistance recipients, lunch programs, child protection service cases, mortality rates, mental health and substance abuse information, suicide rates, law enforcement data.

Step 5: Present the document to your supervisor. Do not presenting anything that needs to be approved by the Institutional Review Board (IRB) or through other organizations. It is no secret that staring at a document too long leaves room for error.

WARNING: Do not skip Step 5. Do not publicly release private information from an organization, or present data that they wish to present themselves. This would be detrimental to your cause and may turn them away from joining your efforts. ALWAYS protect your stakeholders, providers, and community members.

Step 6: Attend community meetings. There are numerous committees and organizations that come together to focus on strengthening the community. Become involved in these meetings and make it a priority to attend as many as possible. This will help you stay current on all the initiatives within the community and introduce you as well. You have met one-on-one with some of these individuals but not all of them. You will have the opportunity to meet community members, small business owners, and liaisons that could be of great assistance to you.

Important meetings to attend: community chamber of commerce meeting, community service council meeting, city council meeting, United Way meeting, Rotary Club meeting, school board meeting, substance abuse prevention council meeting, early childhood development meeting, and mental health taskforce meeting. You can always branch out to Lions Club meetings, Kiwanis, local fire department meetings, health department meetings, etc. It is most important to attend those meetings directly related to your cause first, and then add other meetings as time moves forward.

REMEMBER: While attending these meetings, be sure to network with all present. This is where your business cards are crucial. Pass them out to anyone and everyone, while giving them a brief description of who you are and your initiative. Be sure to collect their business cards as well. If they do not have one, write down their e-mail addresses. Once you get back to your office, e-mail these individuals. Remind them of your effort and see if they can meet with you. Use the sample e-mail from step 2 of this chapter or create your own.

Tip: Think of this as if you are courting the organization or individual. Remember, relationship building is pivotal to your community success. These are great steps to take and with your own special touch, will be the key to your success. The community wants to get to know the true you, so be yourself and shine bright!

Chapter Two: Your First Meeting

With the frequency of one-on-one meetings slowing down, the regularity of your community meeting schedule, and the completion of your community assessment, you are ready to begin the next stage of your work. Remember, you may be staging, but all of these new relationships require continual nurturing. This is your responsibility. You will need to maintain these relationships as you continue to network, and build even more relationships.

First meeting

With your internal support in place, community assessment complete and community relationships developing, it is time to make a move and hold your first coalition meeting. This will bring together all your new connections, both organizations and individuals. This is a "make it or break it" event. The purpose is to leave the group excited and energized to work toward your cause. I say "your" cause now, but if done correctly, it will become their cause.

Step 1: *Location, Location, Location*: Identify a location where you can hold monthly meetings. There are many places within a community that offer large rooms, free of charge. So, get out there and find them. Be strategic about this location. Consider the growth of your group, and that some community members may not be comfortable in certain locations such as churches, schools, courthouses, etc. Once you locate a venue, book it for 12 months.

REMEMBER: (1) Consistency is vital. Know the date, time, and location of your meetings for the next year based off the date, time, and location of your first meeting. (2) Your meeting day and time should change ONLY if your group requests it. If attendance is low, take a poll and see if a new time or day would help.

Examples of locations: Libraries, school administration buildings, local YMCAs, local hospitals, and community colleges. Be sure to find a location that allows for growth and is neutral.

Step 2: Create excitement: When planning your first coalition meeting, think about who in your internal support system is energetic, charismatic, passionate, and experienced. This is the person you want to present your cause at the first meeting. You want to energize the room, stimulate thinking, and get individuals excited. It is not that you are boring, but an individual with a vast amount of knowledge will help with thought-provoking conversation and when answering difficult questions.

Example: Use employer-aided assistance. This may be your supervisor, the CEO of your company, or free state assistance. They are relatable, energetic, and experienced on the needs throughout the community.

Step 3: Create a contact list: Comb over every e-mail correspondence. Use this information to create a list of potential attendees to your first meeting. Invite ALL the individuals you have met over the past few weeks or months. Just like any event, you cannot expect all will attend, so the more you invite the higher the attendance.

Tip: Keep an Excel spread sheet list of all contacts you have made. This creates an organized record of everyone to invite to future meetings.

Step 4: *Create an event*: In your e-mail calendar, create an event to be forwarded to all on your contact list. Add all the details of the meeting to this invitation. You want to include: time, date, location, guest speakers, if lunch is provided, topics, your contact information, and so on.

Tip: Remain mindful of the meeting time. If it is a lunch-hour time slot, you may want to provide lunch, same goes for a dinner-hour time slot. You will not gain the attendance desired if you do not remain cognizant of these details.

Sample: E-mail invitation to a coalition meeting:

I am pleased to invite you to the first Johnson County Coalition Meeting. I look forward to bringing together everyone working within our community to create change. Lunch will be provided.

Please RSVP as soon as possible so we are penciled in AND there is enough food for all!

**If you know anyone you feel would be a good fit for the coalition, please invite them! I look forward to seeing you all there.

Coalition meeting details
When: November 16, 2016.
       11:30 a.m.-12:30 p.m.
Where: Johnson County Administration Building
       34 W. 7th. Street, Littleton, MN. 67850
       (In the basement)

Topics: Why we have all come together to build the coalition* Guest speaker James Smith, Director of Thomas Flight Hospital.

***Contact Sarah Sawyer at (123) 456-7898 with any questions.

Step 5: *Send the invitation and track responses*: It is important you track who responds to your invitation to the meeting. Follow this step each month. By keeping track of the responses, you can (1) Reach out to those without a response prior to the meeting, and discuss if they can attend. (2) Ensure you have enough food, agenda's, and seating for all.

Tip: As you track monthly responses, you can identify who consistently attends the meetings and who does not. Once these individuals are identified, you can reach out to them and voice your desire to have them or a representative attend. It is important to maintain open communication and some level of expectation. Attendance will diminish if you do not maintain relationships.

Chapter Three: Being Prepared

This chapter is all about preparing for your first community meeting. There are a lot of details that need to be thought of and managed. You want to make sure this is a huge success for you and most importantly, your community. *Remember*, you have spent quality time courting and encouraging community members to get involved. Show those community members that you are organized and professional.

Step 1: *Create and print off copies of the meeting agenda*: The agenda is an important tool to help keep you on task. This document will assist in reminding you of important topics to cover during the meeting.

If you have never created an agenda before, make sure to include all items listed below. You do have creative freedom here, however, always remain professional and to the point.

Name of the coalition (if you do not have one, create a generic one for now)
Date and time of the meeting
Topics to be discussed
Meeting facilitator(s)
Bulleted topics and time increments expected on each
Date and time of next meeting
Information for providing meeting feedback

Tip #1: Be consistent with the meeting day and time. If your meeting day falls on the second Wednesday of the month, try to have each meeting thereafter on the second Wednesday of each month. This way you can get the individuals in attendance on a schedule. A consistent schedule ensures consistent attendance.

REMEMBER: If your coalition requests a change in meeting time or date, listen and make desired changes.

Tip #2: Print at least five extra copies of your agenda, as some individuals will not RSVP and you want to be prepared.

Tip #3: Provide the next meeting date and information for meeting feedback on your agenda. This will help you improve your meeting attendance, performance, and encourage the sharing of new topics to discuss.

Sample meeting agenda:

Change Coalition Meeting Agenda
November 16, 2016- 11:30 a.m.-12:30 p.m.
Topics to be discussed: Why we have come together, an open coalition discussion on motivation to change.

Meeting Facilitators: James Smith, Director of Thomas Flight Hospital and Sarah Sawyer, Johnson County Community Coordinator.

  I. Introductions of all in attendance. Secretarial volunteer to take notes (five minutes)

 II. James Smith- Introduction to why we have come together (40 minutes)

III. Discussion about needs and who is missing from this meeting. Who you want to see in December? (15 minutes)

Send meeting feedback to Sarah Sawyer at
ssawyer@cmhc.org

or call (123) 456-7898

NEXT MEETING IS DECEMBER 14, 2016

_@ 11:30 A.M.-12:30 P.M._

Step 2: Create and print off a sign-in sheet. A sign-in sheet should be passed around and signed by everyone in attendance every month. It should include the following:

Name of the group meeting
Name of the meeting facilitator
The date the meeting was held
Area for attendee name, organization, phone and e-mail information.

Sample meeting sign-in sheet:

Change Coalition Meeting Sign-In Sheet
Facilitator:
Date:

Name	Organization	Phone	E-Mail

Step 3: Order the catering. Find out your monthly budget for catering and stay within those means. Once that has been established, identify some local area restaurants that might provide lunch for your meeting.

Once you have identified where you would like to order, make sure they are open for operation during your meeting hours. Some restaurants may not open before noon, and are not options if your meeting is at 11:30 a.m.

Order your catering at least three days in advance. The sooner you order, the better. Be sure to have the pick-up time about 30-45 minutes prior to the meeting start time. Account for waiting, drive time, and set up.

Tip #1: You will want to ensure that the catering is not messy, is easy to eat, and is DELICIOUS! Do not serve less than desirable food to your attendees.

Tip #2: If you do not have a catering budget, and lunch will not be provided, explain that to attendees ahead of time. Add this detail to your meeting invitation and encourage attendees to bring their lunch. I used the term "meet and eat" once catering was no longer provided at the meetings I facilitated.

Step 4: Get it all together: Get all your agenda's and sign-in sheets stapled, filed and in one place the night before the meeting. Once all your documents are organized, place them in your car. This may sound crazy, but it may prevent you from worrying that you forgot something.

Tip: Pack extra pens, and a pad of paper. You will need the pens for the sign-in sheet and the paper for your note-taker.

Chapter Four: The Big Day

The day of your first coalition meeting has finally arrived, and if you are anything like I was you are a wreck. Try not to be nervous about today, as you are prepared and ready to go! This chapter will walk you through the day and how to ensure every meeting after this one is more and more successful.

Step 1: Pick up your catering: Arrive at the designated pick-up time, with cash or your debit card. Sign for your order, get the receipt and take the food to your car. Be sure to keep your receipt. Depending on your employer, you may be able to use the receipt to get reimbursed for this purchase.

Step 2: Arrive early: Be sure to arrive at your meeting location between 30-45 minutes before the start time. Use this time to set up the catering, arrange the room to suit your needs, and place agendas in front of each chair.

Step 3: Arrange the catering to suit your needs: I always use a big table in the back, like a buffet. This way the guests can see what is offered and move through the line in a uniform manner.

Step 4: Arrange the seating to suit your meeting needs: I always used a circle. This way everyone can see each other and participate in the conversation.

Step 5: Arrange Public Address (PA) needs for your guest speaker: Be sure your speaker is comfortable and has all the things s/he needs. This may be a large monitor, microphone or large drawing pads. Everything depends on the topic and method of delivery.

Tip: If you do not know how to work the PA system, ASK SOMEONE! You will find that people are always willing to help, especially if they are hosting the meeting in their building.

Step 6: Greetings: As your attendees arrive, be sure to greet each and every one by name. Smile, shake their hands, and express your gratitude for their attendance. Your relationship with them is extremely important and must remain at the forefront.

REMEMBER: Have everyone sign-in as they arrive to the meeting. You can also pass the sign-in sheet around the table after everyone has found their seat.

Step 7: Start your meeting on time: If your agenda says 11:30 a.m., be sure to begin at 11:30 a.m. Time is valuable. The individuals in attendance want to know you respect their time. Call the meeting to order and begin to work your agenda. Stay mindful of the time and keep your attendees on task.

Step 8: End your meeting on time: If your agenda says the meeting will end at 12:30 p.m., be sure to end at 12:30 p.m. Again, time is valuable, and the individuals in attendance want to know you respect their time.
Tip: Use the final minutes of your meeting to allow for networking. This is a wonderful opportunity for you to mingle with attendees, network further, and open the room up for others to do the same. Everyone enjoys

networking, meeting new people, and learning about new programs in the community.

Step 9: Clean up: Leave the meeting space in the same shape you found it. Be respectful of the organizations space. Show them you are responsible, reliable, and considerate of their organization.

Tip: Consider creating a "who's missing" document and a "needs not met" document. Place these documents on the tables at your meeting and ask the group to fill them out. Use the names and information they provide to reach out, meet new individuals, and invite new organizations to attend your next monthly meeting.

The first meeting is important to your cause. It is the beginning of your effort. Thank everyone for their time. Be sure they leave feeling as though they have accomplished something.

Chapter Five: Now What?

The meeting is over, you cleared the room, and your adrenaline has subsided. Now what? It is time to head back to the office and get things prepared for next month. Go over the sign-in sheet, the minutes taken by your kind volunteer, and prepare your Outlook invitation for next month.

Step 1: Sign-in sheet: Use this sign-in sheet to create a member contact list in Excel. Enter all in attendance and include yourself in the list. Organize all information by: Name, title, organization, phone contact, and e-mail address.

Tip: Update this monthly with new attendees, to help keep count of how many individuals you have hosted.

Step 2: Minutes: Type your meeting minutes the day of the meeting. It is important that you add any details the note-taker may have left out.

Step 3: Invitation: Create an Outlook invitation for next month's meeting, and send it to everyone on your sign-in sheet PLUS everyone you previously invited. It is important to keep the invitation open and grow your contact list.

Tip: Copy and paste the body of your first invitation into the body of the new invitation. Simply change the date and topics to fit the next meeting. This will save you time!

Step 4: _Bulk e-mail_: Create a bulk e-mail with all addresses you used for the Outlook invitation. Attach the newly created member contact list, meeting minutes, and any other information collected at the meeting to the e-mail. Name the subject line: "Coalition meeting minutes and member contact list". Be sure to type a "thank you" message in the body of the e-mail. Thank all who attended and encourage them to come back the following month. Then hit send!

Sample: Thank you message after the first meeting:
Hello coalition group,

 Thank you all for attending the meeting today. It was amazing to see how many in our community are eager to work toward change. I have attached the meeting minutes, and newly created member contact list. If you see any corrections that need to be made or have meeting feedback, please do not hesitate to reach out.

I have also sent an Outlook invitation for next month's meeting. I am hopeful you will all RSVP as soon as possible to ensure the meeting is penciled into your schedule, and that there is enough food for all.

Thank you,
Sarah Sawyer, BS

Feel proud that you accomplished your first community meeting. You successfully brought individuals together. You are at the beginning of a journey that can take you anywhere you want to go.

Chapter Six: Low Hanging Fruit

You spent a few months learning about your community. You built relationships with stakeholders. You hosted community meetings to find common ground. Now is the time to identify "low hanging fruit". What I mean by "low hanging fruit" is small changes that can be easily made, that bring cohesion to the group and a sense of accomplishment.

Tip: Use your community assessment here. It will help you identify small gaps that are easily filled.

Some successful examples of "low hanging fruit" identified by myself and the Miami County Systems Of Care Governance Coalition are listed below.

Digital community resource guide: A digital guide that listed EVERY resource within our community. This guide was previously only available in hard copy. As the technological age continues to take over, we found that access to the resource guide was limited to those who had the means to print the 20-page document.

By transforming the document into an alphabetical guide on the city website, it became available to anyone with computer access. A PDF of the document remained on the chamber website so anyone who wanted a hard copy could print it as desired. To find the digital guide visit www.cityofperu.org

Free trainings: As the coordinator, I identified free trainings open to the community, and forwarded that information to the coalition. This not only informed them of what was available, but provided an opportunity to attend. I encourage you to attend trainings with your coalition members. This shows that you are interested in what you are presenting, and gives you an opportunity to gather ideas for future coalition presentations.

Tip: If you do attend trainings with members of your coalition, encourage them to provide updates to the other members, rather than yourself. This opens dialogue within the group and provides feedback from their peers.

Guest speakers: I identified new or up and coming programs within the community. I invited their directors to present to the coalition. This educated the group on new programs AND prevented me from having to do a majority of the talking.

Guest speaker ideas:
1. The county coroner. S/He always has an interesting perspective on epidemics within the community.
2. Other coalitions from your region. These groups may be working on projects you could collaborate on or work toward tailoring to your community.
3. Senior students with graduation projects. Their projects may be about current issues within the community that your group needs to know about.

Chapter Seven: Assessing Community Needs

Working within a coalition for several months, enabled you to successfully identify "low hanging fruit", and celebrate some small wins. Now it is time to identify the larger needs within your community.

This is done through a well-created and implemented community needs assessment. A community needs assessment is a questionnaire designed and distributed within a community to collect data. This data is then compiled, analyzed and used to identify gaps in resources and/or services within the community of distribution.

Creating a community needs assessment takes time, and therefore be sure you are thorough. Here is where your diverse, educated, and hardworking coalition comes in. There is no need to try and do this alone. You have a dynamic group of individuals eager to help. Take the steps below to make this a successful endeavor.

Step 1: The coalition: Have the conversation with your coalition. Listen to the issues presented daily within their organization. With a large, dynamic group, you will get an array of viewpoints and ideas as to what are the major needs within your community.

Step 2: Identify a theme: After your conversation with the coalition, identify a theme for your assessment. Is there a specific question you all want answered? Is there a pressing need in your community? Use those questions and information to identify the direction of your needs assessment.

Examples of themes for a community needs assessment: Mental health, substance abuse, homelessness, poverty, transportation, workforce development, education, and veteran affairs.

Step 3: Build questions: Your coalition has identified a theme, and an idea of what they want to know. It is time to build questions that may provide the answer. Encourage your coalition to write out as many questions that relate to your topic. No question is wrong at this point.

Step 4: Refine the questions: Your group needs to select the questions most representative of your theme, and the data you wish to collect. After selecting the questions, refine and re-write them if needed. Be sure all questions asked will have the best possibility of providing the answer needed.

Tip #1: You may want to create a work group of about five individuals from the coalition. They will help sort through the questions and build the assessment for the members to review.

Tip 2: Questions that are too long may get skipped, and those with multiple answers may lead to confusion.

Step 5: Build the survey: After the questions have been gone over, re-written, and selected for the final draft; it is time to build the survey. Your group should make sure the survey flows well and is easy to read. Include a cover letter if requested. The letter will explain the purpose of your survey and that all information will remain anonymous.

Tip #1: Keep the survey as short as possible. Asking pertinent questions. Some participants may get bored if the survey is too long.

Tip #2: Use a free survey building software tool for your assessment. There is no need to spend any money. Try a site like www.eSurv.org or www.surveymonkey.com

On the next two pages are examples of a cover sheet and community needs assessment survey. The survey was built by the Miami County Systems Of Care Governance Coalition using www.eSurv.org and has a substance abuse and mental health theme.

Both a link and hard copy of the survey was made available to coalition members distributing within the community.

Change Coalition

34 W. 7th Street Littleton, MN. 67850
Community Needs Assessment Survey
January 2017

Dear Participating Families,

The Change Coalition is conducting a community needs assessment survey to help us identify needs within the community. The data collected will help us to create and or improve substance abuse and mental health programs.

Please take a few minutes to answer the enclosed **confidential questionnaire** about your experiences regarding substance abuse and mental health treatment within our community. Individual answers **will not be disclosed** and will be combined with other community members' surveys.

Please complete and return the questionnaire by February 6, 2017. Thank you in advance for your feedback. It is our hope that this survey will advance positive changes within Johnson County.

Thank you!

1. Please specify your gender:

Female   Male

2. Please specify your age range:

Under 18   18-24   25-34   35-44   45-54   55-64
65+

3. What is the highest degree or level of school you have completed?

Currently enrolled in high school or an equivalency program
Some high school, no diploma
High school graduate or the equivalent
Currently enrolled in a college program
Some college credit, no degree
Trade/technical/vocational training
Associate degree (2 year)
Bachelor's degree (4 year)
Master's degree (6 year) or higher
Prefer not to answer

4. What is your marital status? Please choose one that best fits your current situation.

Single, never married
Married or domestic partnership
Widowed
Divorced
Separated
Prefer not to answer

5. Please specify your current employment status:

Employed for wages
Self-employed
Out of work and looking for work

Out of work but not currently looking for work
A homemaker
Military
A student
Retired
Unable to work
Prefer not to answer

If you answered "Out of work and looking for work" or "Out of work but not currently looking for work" is this due to a felony on your criminal record?

6. Do you believe if your criminal record were expunged (removed completely) you may find employment?
I do not have a criminal record that effects my ability to gain employment
No
Yes
Prefer not to answer

If you answered "Yes" does a lack of funding for, or education on, expungement prevent you from filing?

7. Have you ever participated in any form of a mental health program? (Grief counseling, life coaching, individual therapy, medication, etc.)
No   Yes   Prefer not to answer

If you answered "Yes" to question 7, please specify what mental health program and how you were referred to services (family member, probation/court, doctor, etc.) leave blank if you prefer not to answer.

8. Do you feel the community provides effective treatment for individuals with mental health needs?
No   Yes   Prefer not to answer

If you answered "No" to question 8, what would you like to see improved or made available for those participating in mental health treatment? Please answer below or leave blank if you prefer not to answer.

9. Do you feel as though there is a substance or prescription medication use/abuse issue in Johnson County?
No   Yes   Prefer not to answer

If you answered "Yes" to question 9, which substance (s) or prescription medication (s) do you feel are of most concern? Please answer below or leave blank if you prefer not to answer.

10. Have you ever used an illegal substance or a prescription medication not prescribed to you?

Never taken an illegal substance

Yes, I have taken an illegal substance

Never taken a prescription medication that was not prescribed to me

Yes, I have taken a prescription medication that was not prescribed to me

I have taken both an illegal substance and a prescription medication not prescribed

If you answered "Yes" to question 10, please list the illegal substances and/or prescription medications you have used. Leave blank if you prefer not to answer.

11. Have you ever become addicted to a prescription medication that was prescribed to you for short term pain management of an injury or surgery?

No   Yes   Prefer not to answer

If you answered "Yes" to question 11, did you ever purchase the medication illegally once your prescription expired? Please answer below or leave blank if you prefer not to answer.

12. Have you ever participated in a substance use/abuse treatment program?

No   Yes   I prefer not to answer

If you answered "Yes" to question 12, please specify below which program and how you were referred to services (family member, probation/court, Department of Child Services, etc.) Please leave blank if you prefer not to answer.

13. Have you participated in more than one (1) substance use/abuse treatment program over your life span?
No   Yes   I prefer not to answer
I have never participated in any substance use/abuse treatment

14. Do you feel the community provides effective treatment for individuals with substance use/abuse needs?
No   Yes   Prefer not to answer

If you answered "No" to question 14, please explain below what you would like to see improved or made available when participating in substance use/abuse treatment.

15. Have you been exposed to traumatic events in your lifetime?

No   Yes   Prefer not to answer

If you answered "Yes" to question 15, has it had a negative effect on your life in any way? Please answer below or leave blank if you prefer not to answer.

16. Do you feel as though trauma is understood by service providers within the community?   No   Yes
Somewhat   I do not know   Prefer not to answer

If you answered "No" or "Somewhat" to question 16, what do you feel could help service providers better understand trauma? Please answer below or leave blank if you prefer not to answer.

17. Do you have children?

No   Yes   Prefer not to answer

18. If you answered "Yes" to having children, which answer best
describes your participation level in your child (ren's) lives?

Do not have children   Above average   Average
Below average   Prefer not to answer

19. If you could create a program within the community, based off an original idea or current program in another area, what would it be?

20. Please specify your zip code

Step 6: Implement the survey: After you have spent weeks building your community assessment, it is time to implement it. Your coalition will be a wonderful asset in this process.

Make a list of all coalition members, and their potential distribution locations to map out where to distribute the survey. This will enable you to determine if the distribution locations will result in a proportionate sample. Agree on a length of time the survey is available to participants. The longer the time limit, the more responses you will receive.

Sample: Ideas for survey distribution locations

High Schools- Accessible to faculty, parents, and students. Ask about distributing a link and discuss with teacher's possible extra credit point or two for completion.

Churches: Accessible to staff, volunteers, youth group, and congregation. Ask the Pastor to distribute.

Probation Offices: Accessible to staff, and clients. Ask about distributing to clients daily.

Community Mental Health Centers: Accessible to staff, and clients. Ask if Intensive Outpatient Program (IOP) attendees, therapy facilitators and case managers can ask clients to complete the survey before classes or sessions begin.

Food Pantries: Accessible to volunteers, and staff. Ask if volunteers can distribute the survey for two hours a day for one week. This prevents duplication.

Alternative High School Campuses: Accessible to faculty, parents, and students. Ask about distributing a link and discuss with teachers about a possible extra credit point or two for completion.

County Jail: Accessible to staff, and clients. Ask jail staff if they can ask inmates to complete the survey before classes or sessions begin.

Entire City: Ask the mayor about adding a link to the survey on the city webpage. Have coalition members send out links to all their friends and family, as well as other business acquaintances who live in the county.

<u>Department of Child Services</u>: Accessible to staff, and clients. Ask about distributing a link to Family Case Managers.

<u>Local Organizations</u>: Accessible to staff, and clients. Ask about distributing the survey to potential clients from 9 a.m.–12 p.m. One day the business is open This prevents duplication.

<u>YMCA</u>: Accessible to community.

<u>Hospitals</u>: Accessible to staff and patients.

<u>Adult Education</u>: Distribute to students and faculty.

<u>United Way</u>: Distribute to stakeholders and staff.

<u>AA/NA/AL-ANON</u>: Distribute survey to meeting participants and Al-Anon families.

<u>Mental Health Providers</u>: Distribute to clients.

<u>Early Childhood Organizations</u>: Distribute to families.

<u>Tip #1</u>: Do not target one demographic over another. The survey should be distributed evenly throughout the community.

<u>Step 7</u>: Gather the results: Now that the survey is closed, you have A TON of data to compile. The wonderful thing about eSurv.org is that the website tallies all the data for you. So···if you only provided electronic access to the survey, your job is done. However, if your community is anything like mine, you used paper and a lot of it. The use of paper means that you need to create an Excel sheet or other data collection software, and manually

enter your survey information. This will take time and patience. Did I mention time? Be sure you do not rush this step. Your data should be a true reflection of your assessment.

Step 8: _Analyzing:_ After the survey is closed and the data is tallied, it is time to print the results and analyze. I encourage you to analyze the data with your coalition. Share the results. This will guide you to the next move.

Chapter Eight: Implementation and Strategic Planning

The data analyzed from your community needs assessment should identify some key areas of need within your community. It is what you do with this data that will have the most impact on your community and your coalition. Once your needs are identified, it is time to develop implementation and strategic plans. This will guide your coalition over the next 24-36 months, and keep your actions aligned with your goals.

Step 1: Identify needs from assessment: Once the data has been analyzed, identify top needs. The needs you find may range from transportation to food insecurity; and may even be things you did not suspect.

Tip: To ensure you keep things in scope, choose the top three or top five needs from the assessment. This keeps things from becoming too large, or too small for your coalition.

Step 2: Discuss findings with your coalition: Now that the data has been analyzed, have a group discussion about the results. This conversation will not only help you better understand what data was collected, but will help identify a general direction for the group to follow. The discussion will help you further identify resources that may be underutilized, new, or simply forgotten.

Tip: Work smarter not harder. Do not "recreate the wheel," just improve it. If, in the course of this research, you discover that another coalition is working on an identified top need, consider collaboration. Perhaps your group can assist with strategy to get their program up to its full potential. This will encourage and strengthen community ties, divide the workload, and make it easier to accomplish goals.

Step 3: *Create an implementation plan*: Now that your group has discussed the findings of your data, it is time to organize it in a way that works. Use an excel spreadsheet or something similar to map out each need. Identify the following: Desired outcome, population of focus, strategies, measured outcomes (steps to reaching the goal), who is responsible, time line for the project, status of the project, and how to determine when the plan is complete.

On the next page, is an example of beginning to break a large goal down into measured outcomes; to reach a specific desired outcome. In this case, it is generational poverty that has been selected.

Key factors associated with generational poverty can be survival rather than long-term planning, hopelessness, and contrasting familial value mindset. With these key factors in mind, it is through education and support to other programs that the group felt the best way to reach their goal.

Change Coalition need: GENERATIONAL POVERTY

Desired Outcome: To heal and prevent generational poverty.

Population of focus: All youth and families.

Strategy: Education	
Step 1: Support College Career Success Coalition	
Measured Outcome: *Increased student/parent awareness of class requirements needed for college. *Support all future campus events promoting higher education for students.	Who is responsible? Vocational training organizations Financial Aid Office High School Counselors
Step 2: Support parental/health nurturing programs currently available in community	
Measured Outcome: *Increased attendance to parental/nutrition classes currently in community. *Increase in wellness visits (prevention visits) to health providers. *Decrease in the use of resources over time (HUD, SNAP, TANF)	Who is responsible? Family Social Services Administration United Way Early Childhood Education

Step 4: Vote and agree on the implementation plan: Because relationships, engagement and support are so important, you MUST vote on this plan before putting it into place. This ensures you have full support of the group, and they are invested in the plan. This is your compass for the next 24-36 months, so make sure its leading you in the right direction.

Once the implementation plan is agreed upon, it is time to create a sustainability plan. Sustainability plans focus on how an organization will achieve goals identified, and include program funding opportunities, membership growth, marketing ideas, and much more.
Set this up the same as your implementation plan.

REMEMBER: the implementation and strategic plan is a living document, or a document that can be amended. Nothing about this document is cemented in stone and required to stay as is.

Chapter Nine: Getting to Work

With your newly built compass, your coalition is now ready to get to work. You have several small wins under your belt, and are headed for larger victories. This is where all of the creative minds in your group need to collectively build innovative programs for your community.

You can support other organizations in evidence-based practices, or you can try new things that have the potential to change the lens in which your community views support.

Listed below is one of the innovative programs created within my community. This untraditional program changed the way organizations viewed resources in our community and how they could work toward positive change together.

Life Cycle- A transportation effort that was created to provide a solution to the transportation issue within the rural community of Miami County, IN. The issues being that transportation within Miami County is limited and interferes with the ability to attend daily appointments, as well as hold steady employment. Life Cycle provides a solution to the transportation barrier through the repair and distributing of unclaimed bicycles to needy residents; free of charge. The following pages pose as a "how to" guide on launching this program within any city.

Any community looking to launch this program will need to identify the following:

Bicycles as transportation:

I. Does your community have unclaimed/stolen bicycles?
If so

    a. On average, how many are confiscated/collected each year?
    b. Who is responsible for confiscating/collecting the bicycles?
    c. Where do they store them and for how long?
    d. Is there currently a local government mandate or law surrounding how long a bicycle must be held before "disposed of"? If so, how long does the mandate say the bike must be held, and can that be changed to fit the program needs?

Getting the repairs:

II. Does your community have a local bicycle repair shop? If so

    a. Would the owner of the repair shop be interested in participating in this program?
    b. Will the owner of the repair shop be interested in donating his/her time to the program free of charge? If not, what will they charge you for their time?
    c. How much is average part cost for bicycle repair at their shop, and does that fit in your program budget?
    d. Will the bicycle shop agree to a max repair cost per bicycle?
    e. Will the repair shop sell you bike locks at cost or for a set price?

f. What will the payment schedule be for the repairs?

g. Will the bicycle repair shop be able to deliver the bikes to the access site as needed? If not, who will be responsible for delivery?

h. How will community donations be managed and documented if a community member donates a bike or monies to the bicycle repair shop after hearing about the program?

i. Do you have another repair option should your bicycle repair shop choose not to participate or future issues arise?

Access for the community:

III. *Does your community have a local church or business that would be interested in being the access site for the bicycles? If so*

a. Is this location easily accessible to those with no transportation?

b. Will the organization house the bicycles free of cost? If not, how much will they charge you per month to house the bicycles?

c. Will the organization agree to specific program hours, ensuring the bikes are accessible at least one time per week or as needed in emergency situations?

d. Will this organization allow you to use their 501 (c)(3) to house funds? If not, who will?

e. How will community donations be managed and documented if a community member donates a bike or monies to the access site after hearing about the program?

Liability:
IV. *Is your local government aware of the program and supportive? If so*

    a. Is the city attorney supportive of overlooking the waiver document and program outline to ensure the protection of all agencies participating in the program?

    b. Is local government aware that as the program gains momentum, the need for bike racks and bike lanes may need to be addressed; protecting resident safety and property.

Program Development:

V. *Is everyone on board? If so*

    a. Create a work group of the individuals who will be (1) Collecting the unclaimed/stolen bikes. (2) Repairing the unclaimed/stolen bikes. (3) Acting as the access site for the unclaimed/stolen bikes. (4) Housing the funding for the program (if different from access site) and (5) Law literate to ensure the program waiver is accurate and inclusive of all needs.

    b. Use your lawyer to ensure you have your waiver accurate and complete.

    c. Ensure you have legal access to the unclaimed/stolen bikes by reading the mandate for your community. If there is not one, you will need to request one from the city council. Sixty (60) day hold before releasing to program is appropriate.

    d. Identify the program day, hours and if there will be an "as needed" option for those who need transportation outside of the weekly program hours.

    e. Identify an individual from this group as an executive director of the program. They will be able to make executive decisions should they arise.

    f. Identify eligibility requirements for the program. Age, residency, ID requirements, will then need to have a referral? who will you accept a referral from? will they only be able to access the program once in a lifetime or will you let residents access it more than once? Will there be a waiver? Will the waiver have to be signed independently or can someone sign for the recipient? Will you supply helmets?

Funding and sustainability:
VI. *How will you fund and sustain this effort?*

    a. Identify all local foundations and clubs in which have grant funds available.

    b. Identify any larger state grants that fund innovative transportation initiatives.

    c. Build a program budget with justification that reflects ALL program cost.

    d. Build a program "pitch". One you can take to the local foundations and clubs. They will want to hear about the program AND ask you questions pertaining to the program. Include an outline of your collaborating agencies, program structure, budget with justification, how it benefits the community, how impactful donor dollars will be, projected impact, local stats on transportation issues, independence, privacy and accountability provided by such program. Future growth potential of the program, and how you will sustain it outside of grant funding in the future.

    e. WRITE YOUR GRANTS and begin to request to visit local club meetings. You will want to gain the support of as many individuals as possible.

Marketing:

VII. *Once you gain funding create a marketing strategy to get the word out about the new program.*

    a. Visit local agencies and inform them of your program

    b. Create flyers and post them in local agencies.

    c. Go on the radio and announce the program

    d. Send a flyer to everyone on your e-mail list

    e. Use social media to promote the program

Chapter 10: Creating Policy Within Your Coalition

As your coalition grows, you will find that policies should be set in place to keep meetings and programs running smoothly, as well as define expectations for request from other organizations.

One big question: When to begin building the policy structure, and how to develop it. While every community group is different, be sure to follow the lead of those in your coalition. Listen when members voice likes and dislikes about the current policies within other community councils. The following steps below are helpful as you begin the policy structuring process.

Step 1: Unify the group: Get a few small wins under your belt to create bonding and help unify members. By working in groups, members can get to know one another, create new working relationships and see that they can come together to make a difference within their community. This gives them time to learn to compromise with one another and work out small differences.

Tip: Working together prior to policy creation affords the opportunity to see if members want to remain in the coalition, builds support, and helps generate ideas on how to run the group.

Step 2: Create a mission and vision statement: After you have worked together for some time, create a mission and vision statement. This will encourage further conversation on the direction members wish to work toward and what they hope to see for their community in the years to come.

Mission definition: A formal summary of the aims and values of a company, organization, or individual.

Vision definition: An aspirational description of what an organization would like to achieve or accomplish in the mid-term or long-term future.

While you have an implementation plan, creating a mission and vision statement will help complete the puzzle of what your work will accomplish. If the mission and vision of the group does not align with the initial work it is a time to think about re-evaluating your implementation plan and making adjustments.

Step 3: Write it out: As the group works with one another, they most likely have adopted a way of voting, discussing things, or updating work group progress. Write out these processes to help further the framework to create and implement future policies.

Write out anything, from how the coalition votes in meetings to the structure of work groups and any other processes that mimic policy. If the coalition is already practicing soft policy, the process will be easily accepted and voted in.

Step 4: Bring the group together: After you write out the "soft" policies the group is following, discuss them at a monthly meeting. Present the current framework, identify likes and dislikes of the group about said process, and officially vote it in as policy. Identify and discuss several policy items. Several are listed below:

Membership policy: As membership grows, the question of who is a member will arise making this policy outline a must. Below are several things to decide upon:

(1) How do you become a member of your coalition? (2) How many meetings does a member need to attend yearly to maintain membership? (3) Does a member have to attend meetings *and* be in a workgroup to be considered a member?

Sample: Membership policy: A Change Coalition organization member is an individual or organization that attends at least one half of the yearly meetings and/or participates in one or more of the Change Coalition work groups.

Voting policy: Members will want to make decisions, and that means voting. A policy outlining how to vote will keep things fair and organized as your group grows and moves forward with their work. Below are several things to decide upon:

(1) Who can vote on decisions and/or programs at the meetings? (2) Are members the only ones who can vote on decisions and/or programs? (3) Are votes counted by the number of individuals present at the meeting or by the number of organizations present at the meeting? (4) Will voting be limited to monthly meetings, or will you create a policy for e-mail votes? (5) If you decide on an electronic voting process, who will tally all votes and will those votes be formally recorded?

Sample: Voting policy: The Change Coalition uses a "majority rules" voting policy. A "majority rules" vote is based on (1) The number of organization members present at the meeting, with 51% of those members voting to determine the outcome. (2) An electronic "majority rules" vote based off the number of organization members present at the most recent monthly meeting, with 51% of those members voting to determine the outcome.

Coalition "letter of support" policy: In some cases, your coalition may be sought out by other organizations for a letter of support. Applications procedures for state grants frequently request letters of support from community coalitions, to show collaboration. In the event your coalition is approached for a letter of support from either a member or non-member, a policy created for this process in necessary. Below are several to decide upon.

(1) How will community organizations request letters of support? (2) Will this be through a written request? (3) How many days in advance does the written request need to be submitted? (4) Who will receive the request (5) Is the requesting organization required to present their request to the coalition? (6) Should a standard template for letters of support be created?

Sample: "letter of support" policy: If a non-member organization request documentation of support from the Change Coalition, the requesting organization shall provide verbal or written notification to the coalition chair. The chair then provides a written request of information on the grant or program, possible community benefits, a sustainability plan, and who will provide updates. The chair then adds the following to that information: How many meetings the requesting organization has attended and all collaborative work between that organization and the Change Coalition. This information is then submitted electronically to the Change Coalition co-members for review prior to the monthly meeting. The organization is then placed on the monthly meeting agenda to present further information to co-members and participate in a question and answer session.

If documentation of support is due prior to the Change Coalition's next monthly meeting date, an e-mail vote is then conducted. All information from both the organization and chair is submitted to the Change Coalition electronically, with a "majority rule" vote tallied by the chair, via e-mail in place of the meeting vote. An e-mail vote shall be held open for members to vote for at least five (5) days, excluding Saturdays, Sundays, and legal holidays recognized by the State of Minnesota. If the majority rules in favor of the support, a letter is created, printed, and signed by chair. The chair then provides the document to the requesting organization. The chair shall report the results of the e-mail vote at the next meeting AND the results of the e-mail vote shall be recorded in the meeting minutes.

All documentation of support request are to (1) Be submitted to the chair at least seven (7) days prior to the next scheduled monthly meeting OR ten (10) days prior to the grant deadline, if the grant deadline falls prior to the next meeting. (2) Remains true to the values and/or mission of the Change Coalition. (3) Assists in reaching goals within the implementation and sustainability plan. (4) The receiving organization provides bi-monthly updates to the Change Coalition and member work group participation if requested.

Program support policy: As the coalition grows, more opportunities will arise. Group members may see opportunities for the coalition to attempt new programs. Members may ask the group for support. Create a support policy for members, much like the letter of support policy. This serves as a guide to request support from your group by member organizations. Below are several to decide upon:

(1) How will member organizations request program support from the coalition? (2) Will this be through a written request? (3) How many days in advance will the written request need to be submitted? (4) Who receives the request? (5) Is the member requesting support required to present their request to the coalition? (6) Will a work group need to be created before work begins on project?

Sample: Program support policy: If a Change Coalition member has a program they are interested in implementing, the requesting member provides verbal or written notification to the chair of their interest to receive support from the Change Coalition. The chair then provides a written request to receive an executive summary of information on the program, possible community impact, and a sustainability plan. This information is electronically submitted to co-members for review prior to the next monthly meeting. The organization member is then placed on the monthly meeting agenda. At the meeting, the member will present further information to the co-members and participate in a question and answer session. In the event the group is interested, one motion with one second motion is required with a "majority rule" vote to follow.

If the majority rules in favor of the program, a workgroup is identified and the project is pursued. In the event the majority opposes; the project is denied. All programs and project interests are to (1) Be submitted to the chair at least fourteen (14) days prior to the next scheduled monthly meeting OR thirty (30) days prior to the grant or program deadline (2) Remains true to the values and/or mission of the Change Coalition (3) Assists in reaching goals within the created implementation and sustainability plans. (4) The work group provides updates to the Change Coalition.

Political policies and the coalition: As election season cannot be avoided, your coalition must openly discuss policy concerning political parties, and if candidates can be endorsed through your community group. You will want to consider (1) All laws, should you or any other members work for local, state, or federal governments. Those specific organizations have clear outlines for employee participation in elections.

Sample: Political party policy: As an agency funded through state grant dollars, the Change Coalition may not get involved in political campaign matters. Individual associates are free to choose a political affiliation, but should not represent such parties while representing the Change Coalition.

While these are basic policies, your groups policies will expand and continue to be created specific to the groups needs.

Chapter Eleven: Sustainability

The word sustainability is defined as: The ability to be maintained at a certain rate or level. This means that to sustain your coalition, you will need more than money. Your coalition will need to consider how it will sustain membership, programs, salaries, and momentum as these are imperative to long-term success.

Below are ideas for maintaining each of the items mentioned and continued success for a long time to come.

Step 1: Identify ways to build membership: The more members you have, the more access to resources, ideas, and funding. Your members are the life of the coalition, and it is pertinent to continue to focus on this aspect of sustainability. I encourage you take "your show on the road" and make yourself known in the community.

From chapter one, I have relisted the important meetings you should attend, because you need to present coalition programs at these meetings. Now that progress has been made, share the good news and see if others would like to join in your efforts.

Important meetings to present progress to: Community chamber of commerce meeting, resource committee meeting, city council meeting, United Way meeting, Rotary Club meeting, substance abuse prevention council meeting, early childhood development meeting, and mental health task force meeting.

Step 2: *Sustaining programing:* Now that you have implemented programs, you want to ensure they are maintained and accessible. Several ideas to maintain program sustainability are listed below.

1. Community foundations: Identify any community foundations within your area. These foundations house funding dollars for a magnitude of different projects. Foundations are a great place to start when looking for seed money.
2. Grants: Grants are an amazing resource to find funding for any kind of project or program. A great place to find specific grants to fit your needs is with a simple "Google" search.
3. Local sororities or clubs: Most local sororities and clubs within your community routinely raise funds for charitable causes. These clubs range from the Lions Club to Rotary Club.
4. United Way: Head to your local United Way and meet with their director. S/he is knowledgeable about local resources, grants, foundations, and possible private donors.
5. Faith-based organizations: Faith-based members of your coalition may be open to applying for funding, and contributing those funds to your coalitions programs.

Step 3: *Discuss salary sustainability:* This can be the most difficult conversation to have as none of us like to talk about money. However, we must! If the time has come to discuss financial sustainability of a paid position, below are some direct and indirect ways your group can find funds.

1. Consider "in-kind" fund matches. These can help ease the burden of office space, copies, and meeting locations.
2. Fundraising is another way to ease an organizations financial responsibility when it comes to maintaining a salary.
3. Apply for grants. Applying for grants that pay coordinators a specific salary yearly for their dedication to a cause can help draw funds to the needed position.

Step 4: Keep momentum by identifying new, innovative, and easily implemented programs: Programing creates access, treatment, and change. It is so important to be aware of new programs implemented by other coalitions, providers, or organizations.

A good way to keep up to date is through research. Spend a couple hours a week researching other community coalitions, what has worked for them, and what you may be able to implement in your own community.

Identifying easily implemented changes will increase program success for organizations, while building momentum and confidence for the coalition.

Tip #1: I found success by taking pieces of new programs to see if those pieces could easily fit into current community programs. This created a compliment to the current program and increased successful outcomes without creating large amounts of work.

Tip #2: If you have an innovative idea, do not hesitate to present it to the coalition. Some of the greatest ideas come from the most unlikely places. Whether or not you are afraid of rejection, present your ideas to the coalition. Allow the group to decide whether the program is worthwhile. **You have nothing to lose.**

Conclusion: The Book Ends Here, But Your Work Does Not.

You made it through the last chapter of this book, and are most likely asking "That's it?". I am happy to answer, "No! That's not it." You have so many more opportunities to grow your community group and their efforts far beyond the pages of this book.

The possibilities to develop marketing plans, logos, and policy changes are endless. Becoming more prominent in the community, and recognized as a mobilized organization will provide the attention you need to continue the groups success.

As you move forward on your journey, remember to work smarter not harder, and acknowledge your relationships as the catalyst for your success.

Work closely with those you trust. Find a mentor that can guide you as you grow and develop into your new role as a community coordinator. A mentor will help keep you focused as you implement new ideas and approach the coalition on possible policy changes.

It is also important to have set goals not only for the coalition, but for yourself. Goals will help you grow professionally and have future impact on your community and state. If you have goals outside of community mobilization, continue to pursue them. Personal growth will refine your craft and improve your work within the community.

It is with great hope that these pages will be of assistance in any way as you think about mobilizing your community or breathe new life into a current group. Find where you are, or where you want to be, and begin.

Made in the USA
Las Vegas, NV
15 March 2023

69117991R00049